The War Poets

AN ANTHOLOGY

The War Poets

AN ANTHOLOGY

80 POWERFUL POEMS FROM
THE FIRST WORLD WAR

PITKIN

First published in the United Kingdom
in 2026 by
Pitkin
43 Great Ormond Street
London
WC1N 3HZ

An imprint of B. T. Batsford Holdings Limited

ISBN 978 1 83733 073 7

A CIP catalogue record for this book is available from the British Library.

10 9 8 7 6 5 4 3 2 1

Reproduction by Rival Colour Ltd, UK
Printed and bound by Dream Colour, China

This book can be ordered direct from the publisher at www.batsfordbooks.com, or try your local bookshop.

Distributed throughout the UK and Europe by Abrams & Chronicle Books, 1st Floor, 22–24 Ely Place, London EC1N 6TE and 57 rue Gaston Tessier, 75166 Paris, France

www.abramsandchronicle.co.uk
info@abramsandchronicle.co.uk

Died of Wounds, *Trench Duty*, *The General*, *The Dug-Out*, *To Any Dead Officer*, *Prelude: The Troops*, *Everyone Sang*, *Twelve Months After*, and *Base Details* all by Siegfried Sassoon, reprinted by kind permission of George Sassoon.

FSC
www.fsc.org
MIX
Paper | Supporting responsible forestry
FSC® C188448

CONTENTS

Herbert Asquith

1881–1947. His father was prime minister from 1908–1916.

AFTER THE SALVO

Up and down, up and down,
They go, the gray rat, and the brown.
The telegraph lines are tangled hair,
Motionless on the sullen air;
An engine has fallen on its back,
With crazy wheels, on a twisted track;
All ground to dust is the little town;
Up and down, up and down
They go, the gray rat, and the brown.
A skull, torn out of the graves nearby,
Gapes in the grass. A butterfly,
In azure iridescence new,
Floats into the world, across the dew;
Between the flow'rs. Have we lost our way,
Or are we toys of a god at play,
Who do these things on a young Spring day?

Where the salvo fell, on a splintered ledge
Of ruin, at the crater's edge,
A poppy lives: and young, and fair,
The dewdrops hang on the spider's stair,
With every rainbow still unhurt
From leaflet unto leaflet girt.

Man's house is crushed; the spider's lives:
Inscrutably He takes, and gives,
Who guards not any temple here,
Save the temple of the gossamer.

Up and down, up and down
They go, the gray rat, and the brown:
A pistol cracks: they too are dead.

The nightwind rustles overhead.

Laurence Binyon

1869–1943. For the Fallen is linked with services of remembrance all over the world.

FOR THE FALLEN

With proud thanksgiving, a mother for her children,
England mourns for her dead across the sea.
Flesh of her flesh they were, spirit of her spirit,
Fallen in the cause of the free.

Solemn the drums thrill: Death august and royal
Sings sorrow up into immortal spheres.
There is music in the midst of desolation
And a glory that shines upon our tears.

They went with songs to the battle, they were young,
Straight of limb, true of eye, steady and aglow.
They were staunch to the end against odds uncounted,
They fell with their faces to the foe.

They shall grow not old, as we that are left grow old:
Age shall not weary them, nor the years condemn.
At the going down of the sun and in the morning
We will remember them.

They mingle not with their laughing comrades again;
They sit no more at familiar tables of home;
They have no lot in our labour of the day-time;
They sleep beyond England's foam.

But where our desires are and our hopes profound,
Felt as a well-spring that is hidden from sight,
To the innermost heart of their own land they are known
As the stars are known to the Night;

As the stars that shall be bright when we are dust,
Moving in marches upon the heavenly plain,
As the stars that are starry in the time of our darkness,
To the end, to the end, they remain.

from AIRMEN FROM OVERSEAS

Who are these that come from the ends of the oceans,
Coming as the swallows come out of the South
In the glory of Spring? They are come among us
With purpose in the eyes, with a smile on the mouth.

These are they who have left the familiar faces,
Sights, sounds and scents of familiar land,
Taking no care for security promised aforetime,
Sweetness of home and the future hope had planned.

A lode-star has drawn them; Britain, standing alone
Clear in the darkness, not to be overcome,
Though the huge masses of hate are hurled against her,
Wherever the spirit of freedom breathes, is Home.

Soon they are joined with incomparable comrades,
Britain's flower and Britain's pride,
Against all odds, despising the boastful Terror,
On joyous wings in the ways of the wind they ride.

From afar they battle for our ancient island,
Soaring and pouncing, masters of the skies.
They are heard in the night by lands betrayed and
captive.
And a throbbing of hope to their thunder-throb replies.

To dare incredible things, from the ends of ocean
They are coming and coming, over the perilous seas.
How shall we hail them? Truly there are no words
And no song worthy of these.

p/o David Bourne

Pilot Officer Bourne of the RAFVR was shot down and killed in 1941.

"OPERATIONS CALLING!"

"Clearing Black Section
Patrol Bass Rock,"
Leaps heart; after shock
Action comes stumbling;
Snatch your helmet;
Then run smoothly, to the grumbling
Of a dozing Merlin heating
Supercharged air,
You are there
by "Z"
Down hard on the behind
The parachute; you are blind
With your oxygen snout
But click, click, click, click, you feel
and the harness is fixed.

Round the wing
And "Out of the cockpit, you,"
Clamber the rung
And the wing as if a wasp had stung
You, hop and jump into the cockpit,
Split second to spike
The Sutton harness holes,
One, two, three, four,
Thrust with your
Hand to the throttle open . . .

"Operations" called and spoken.

Rupert Brooke

FRAGMENT

I strayed about the deck, an hour, to-night
Under a cloudy moonless sky; and peeped
In at the windows, watched my friends at table,
Or playing cards, or standing in the doorway,
Or coming out into the darkness. Still
No one could see me.

   I would have thought of them
– Heedless, within a week of battle – in pity,
Pride in their strength and in the weight and firmness
And link'd beauty of bodies, and pity that
This gay machine of splendour 'ld soon be broken,
Thought little of, pashed, scattered. . . .

   Only, always,
I could but see them – against the lamplight – pass
Like coloured shadows, thinner than filmy glass,
Slight bubbles, fainter than the wave's faint light,
That broke to phosphorus out in the night,
Perishing things and strange ghosts – soon to die
To other ghosts – this one, or that, or I.

1914
Selected Sonnets
I. PEACE

Now, God be thanked Who has matched us with His hour,
   And caught our youth, and wakened us from sleeping,
With hand made sure, clear eye, and sharpened power,
   To turn, as swimmers into cleanness leaping,

Glad from a world grown old and cold and weary,
   Leave the sick hearts that honour could not move,
And half-men, and their dirty songs and dreary,
   And all the little emptiness of love!

Oh! we, who have known shame, we have found
   release there,
   Where there's no ill, no grief, but sleep has mending,
      Naught broken save this body, lost but breath;
Nothing to shake the laughing heart's long peace there
   But only agony, and that has ending;
      And the worst friend and enemy is but Death.

II. SAFETY

Dear! of all happy in the hour, most blest
  He who has found our hid security,
Assured in the dark tides of the world that rest,
  And heard our word, 'Who is so safe as we?'
We have found safety with all things undying,
  The winds, and morning, tears of men and mirth,
The deep night, and birds singing, and clouds flying,
  And sleep, and freedom, and the autumnal earth.

We have built a house that is not for Time's throwing.
  We have gained a peace unshaken by pain for ever.
War knows no power. Safe shall be my going,
  Secretly armed against all death's endeavour;
Safe though all safety's lost; safe where men fall;
And if these poor limbs die, safest of all.

IV. THE DEAD

These hearts were woven of human joys and cares,
  Washed marvellously with sorrow, swift to mirth.
The years had given them kindness. Dawn was theirs,
  And sunset, and the colours of the earth.
These had seen movement, and heard music; known
  Slumber and waking; loved; gone proudly friended;
Felt the quick stir of wonder; sat alone;
  Touched flowers and furs and cheeks. All this is ended.

There are waters blown by changing winds to laughter
And lit by the rich skies, all day. And after,
  Frost with a gesture, stays the waves that dance
And wandering loveliness. He leaves a white
  Unbroken glory, a gathered radiance,
A width, a shining peace, under the night.

V. THE SOLDIER

If I should die, think only this of me:
  That there's some corner of a foreign field
That is for ever England. There shall be
  In that rich earth a richer dust concealed;
A dust whom England bore, shaped, made aware,
  Gave, once, her flowers to love, her ways to roam,
A body of England's, breathing English air,
  Washed by the rivers, blest by suns of home.

And think, this heart, all evil shed away,
  A pulse in the eternal mind, no less
    Gives somewhere back the thoughts by England given;
Her sights and sounds; dreams happy as her day;
  And laughter, learnt of friends; and gentleness,
    In hearts at peace, under an English heaven.

THE FUNERAL OF YOUTH: THRENODY

The day that *Youth* had died,
There came to his grave-side,
In decent mourning, from the county's ends,
Those scatter'd friends
Who had lived the boon companions of his prime,
And laughed with him and sung with him and wasted,
In feast and wine and many-crown'd carouse,
The days and nights and dawnings of the time
When *Youth* kept open house,
Nor left untasted
Aught of his high emprise and ventures dear,
No quest of his unshar'd –
All these, with loitering feet and sad head bar'd,
Followed their old friend's bier.
Folly went first,
With muffled bells and coxcomb still revers'd;
And after trod the bearers, hat in hand –
Laughter, most hoarse, and Captain *Pride* with tanned
And martial face all grim, and fussy *Joy*,
Who had to catch a train, and *Lust*, poor snivelling boy;
These bore the dear departed.

Behind them, broken-hearted,
Came *Grief*, so noisy a widow, that all said,
'Had he but wed
Her elder sister *Sorrow*, in her stead!'
And by her, trying to soothe her all the time,
The fatherless children, *Colour*, *Tune*, and *Rhyme*,
(The sweet lad *Rhyme*), ran all-uncomprehending.
Then, at the way's sad ending,
Round the raw grave they stay'd. Old *Wisdom* read
In mumbling tone the Service for the Dead.
There stood *Romance*,
The furrowing tears had mark'd her rougèd cheek;
Poor old *Conceit*, his wonder unassuag'd;
Dead *Innocency's* daughter, *Ignorance*;
And shabby, ill-dress'd *Generosity*;
And *Argument*, too full of woe to speak;
Passion, grown portly, something middle-ag'd;
And *Friendship* – not a minute older, she;
Impatience, ever taking out his watch;
Faith, who was deaf, and had to lean, to catch
Old *Wisdom's* endless drone.
Beauty was there,
Pale in her black; dry-eyed; she stood alone.
Poor maz'd Imagination; *Fancy* wild;

Ardour, the sunlight on his greying hair;
Contentment, who had known *Youth* as a child
And never seen him since. And *Spring* came too,
Dancing over the tombs, and brought him flowers –
She did not stay for long.
And *Truth*, and *Grace*, and all the merry crew,
The laughing *Winds* and *Rivers*, and lithe *Hours*;
And *Hope*, the dewy-eyed; and sorrowing *Song*; –
Yes, with much woe and mourning general,
At dead *Youth's* funeral,
Even these were met once more together, all,
Who erst the fair and living *Youth* did know;
All, except only *Love*. *Love* had died long ago.

THE GREAT LOVER

I have been so great a lover: filled my days
So proudly with the splendour of Love's praise,
The pain, the calm, and the astonishment,
Desire illimitable, and still content,
And all dear names men use, to cheat despair,
For the perplexed and viewless streams that bear
Our hearts at random down the dark of life.
Now, ere the unthinking silence on that strife
Steals down, I would cheat drowsy Death so far,
My night shall be remembered for a star
That outshone all the suns of all men's days.
Shall I not crown them with immortal praise
Whom I have loved, who have given me, dared with me
High secrets, and in darkness knelt to see
The inenarrable godhead of delight?
Love is a flame: – we have beaconed the world's night.
A city: – and we have built it, these and I.
An emperor: – we have taught the world to die.
So, for their sakes I loved, ere I go hence,
And the high cause of Love's magnificence,
And to keep loyalties young, I'll write those names

Golden for ever, eagles, crying flames,
And set them as a banner, that men may know,
To dare the generations, burn, and blow
Out on the wind of Time, shining and streaming …

These I have loved:
  White plates and cups, clean-gleaming,
Ringed with blue lines; and feathery, faery dust;
Wet roofs, beneath the lamp-light; the strong crust
Of friendly bread; and many-tasting food;
Rainbows; and the blue bitter smoke of wood;
And radiant raindrops couching in cool flowers;
And flowers themselves, that sway through sunny hours,
Dreaming of moths that drink them under the moon;
Then, the cool kindliness of sheets, that soon
Smooth away trouble; and the rough male kiss
Of blankets; grainy wood; live hair that is
Shining and free; blue-massing clouds; the keen
Unpassioned beauty of a great machine;
The benison of hot water; furs to touch;
The good smell of old clothes; and other such –
The comfortable smell of friendly fingers,
Hair's fragrance, and the musty reek that lingers

About dead leaves and last year's ferns …
Dear names,
And thousand others throng to me! Royal flames;
Sweet water's dimpling laugh from tap or spring;
Holes in the ground; and voices that do sing:
Voices in laughter, too; and body's pain,
Soon turned to peace; and the deep-panting train;
Firm sands; the little dulling edge of foam
That browns and dwindles as the wave goes home;
And washen stones, gay for an hour; the cold
Graveness of iron; moist black earthen mould;
Sleep; and high places; footprints in the dew;
And oaks; and brown horse-chestnuts, glossy-new;
And new-peeled sticks; and shining pools on grass; –
All these have been my loves. And these shall pass,
Whatever passes not, in the great hour,
Nor all my passion, all my prayers, have power
To hold them with me through the gate of Death.
They'll play deserter, turn with traitor breath,
Break the high bond we made, and sell Love's trust
And sacramented covenant to the dust.
– Oh, never a doubt but, somewhere, I shall wake,
And give what's left of love again, and make
New friends now strangers …

But the best I've known
Stays here, and changes, breaks, grows old, is blown
About the winds of the world, and fades from brains
Of living men, and dies.
Nothing remains.

O dear my loves, O faithless, once again
This one last gift I give: that after men
Shall know, and later lovers, far-removed,
Praise you, "All these were lovely"; say, "He loved."

THE NIGHT JOURNEY

Hands and lit faces eddy to a line;
  The dazed last minutes click; the clamour dies.
Beyond the great-swung arc o' the roof, divine,
  Night, smoky-scarv'd, with thousand coloured eyes

Glares the imperious mystery of the way.
  Thirsty for dark, you feel the long-limbed train
Throb, stretch, thrill motion, slide, pull out and sway,
  Strain for the far, pause, draw to strength again…

– As a man, caught by some great hour, will rise,
  Slow-limbed, to meet the light or find his love;
And, breathing long, with staring sightless eyes,
  Hands out, head back, agape and silent, move

Sure as a flood, smooth as a vast wind blowing;
  And, gathering power and godhead as he goes,
Unstumbling, unreluctant, strong, unknowing,
  Borne by a will not his, that lifts, that grows,

Sweep out to darkness, triumphing to his goal,
   Out of the fire, out of the little room! …
– There is an end appointed, O my soul!
   Crimson and green the signals burn. The gloom

Is hung with steam's fantastic livid streamers.
   Lost into God, as lights in light, we fly,
Grown one with will, end-drunken huddled dreamers.
   The white lights roar; the sounds of the world die;

And lips and laughter are forgotten things.
   Speed sharpens; grows. Into the night, and on,
The strength and splendour of our purpose swings.
   The lamp fade; and the stars. We are alone.

CLOUDS

Down the blue night the unending columns press
  In noiseless tumult, break and wave and flow,
  Now tread the far South, or lift rounds of snow
Up to the white moon's hidden loveliness.
Some pause in their grave wandering comradless,
  And turn with profound gesture vague and slow,
  As who would pray good for the world, but know
Their benediction empty as they bless.

They say that the Dead die not, but remain
  Near to the rich heirs of their grief and mirth.
    I think they ride the calm mid-heaven, as these,
In wise majestic melancholy train,
    And watch the moon, and the still-raging seas,
  And men, coming and going on the earth.

ONE DAY

To-day I have been happy. All the day
  I held the memory of you, and wove
Its laughter with the dancing light o' the spray,
  And sowed the sky with tiny clouds of love,
And sent you following the white waves of sea,
  And crowned your head with fancies, nothing worth,
Stray buds from that old dust of misery,
  Being glad with a new foolish quiet mirth.

So lightly I played with those dark memories,
Just as a child, beneath the summer skies,
  Plays hour by hour with a strange shining stone,
For which (he knows not) towns were fire of old,
  And love has been betrayed, and murder done,
And great kings turned to a little bitter mould.

THE OLD VICARAGE, GRANTCHESTER

(Café des Westerns, Berlin, May 1912)

Although this poem was written before the war, it shows Brooke's great love for England.

Just now the lilac is in bloom,
All before my little room;
And in my flower-beds, I think,
Smile the carnation and the pink;
And down the borders, well I know,
The poppy and the pansy blow …
Oh! there the chestnuts, summer through,
Beside the river make for you
A tunnel of green gloom, and sleep
Deeply above; and green and deep
The stream mysterious glides beneath,
Green as a dream and deep as death.
– Oh, damn! I know it! and I know
How the May fields all golden show,
And when the day is young and sweet,
Gild gloriously the bare feet
That run to bathe …

Du lieber Gott!
Here am I, sweating, sick, and hot,
And there the shadowed waters fresh
Lean up to embrace the naked flesh.
Temperamentvoll German Jews
Drink beer around; – and there the dews
Are soft beneath a morn of gold.
Here tulips bloom as they are told;
Unkempt about those hedges blows
An English unofficial rose;
And there the unregulated sun
Slopes down to rest when day is done,
And wakes a vague unpunctual star,
A slippered Hesper; and there are
Meads towards Haslingfield and Coton
Where *das Betreten*'s not *verboten*.

eithe genoimen … would I were
In Grantchester, in Grantchester! –
Some, it may be, can get in touch
With Nature there, or Earth, or such.
And clever modern men have seen
A Faun a-peeping through the green,
And felt the classics were not dead,

To glimpse a Naiad's reedy head,
Or hear the Goat-foot piping low: ...
But these are things I do not know.
I only know that you may lie
Day long and watch the Cambridge sky,
And, flower-lulled in sleepy grass,
Hear the cool lapse of hours pass,
Until the centuries blend and blur
In Grantchester, in Grantchester ...
Still in the dawnlit waters cool
His ghostly Lordship swims his pool,
And tries the strokes, essays the tricks,
Long learnt on Hellespont, or Styx.

Dan Chaucer hears his river still
Chatter beneath a phantom mill.
Tennyson notes, with studious eye,
How Cambridge waters hurry by ...
And in that garden, black and white,
Creep whispers through the grass all night;
And spectral dance, before the dawn,
A hundred Vicars down the lawn;
Curates, long dust, will come and go
On lissom, clerical, printless toe;

And oft between the boughs is seen
The sly shade of a Rural Dean...
Till, at a shiver in the skies,
Vanishing with Satanic cries,
The prim ecclesiastic rout
Leaves but a startled sleeper-out,
Grey heavens, the first bird's drowsy calls,
The falling house that never falls.

God! I will pack, and take a train,
And get me to England once again!
For England's the one land, I know,
Where men with Splendid Hearts may go;
And Cambridgeshire, of all England,
The shire for Men who Understand;
And of *that* district I prefer
The lovely hamlet Grantchester.
For Cambridge people rarely smile,
Being urban, squat, and packed with guile;
And Royston men in the far South
Are black and fierce and strange of mouth;
At Over they fling oaths at one,
And worse than oaths at Trumpington,
And Ditton girls are mean and dirty,

And there's none in Harston under thirty,
And folks in Shelford and those parts
Have twisted lips and twisted hearts,
And Barton men make Cockney rhymes,
And Coton's full of nameless crimes,

And things are done you'd not believe
At Madingley, on Christmas Eve.
Strong men have run for miles and miles,
When one from Cherry Hinton smiles;
Strong men have blanched, and shot their wives,
Rather than send them to St Ives;
Strong men have cried like babes, bydam,
To hear what happened at Babraham.
But Grantchester! ah, Grantchester!
There's peace and holy quiet there,
Great clouds along pacific skies,
And men and women with straight eyes,
Lithe children lovelier than a dream,
A bosky wood, a slumbrous stream,
And little kindly winds that creep
Round twilight corners, half asleep.
In Grantchester their skins are white;
They bathe by day, they bathe by night;

The women there do all they ought;
The men observe the Rules of Thought.
They love the Good; they worship Truth;
They laugh uproariously in youth;
(And when they get to feeling old,
They up and shoot themselves, I'm told) …

Ah, God! to see the branches stir
Across the moon at Grantchester!
To smell the thrilling-sweet and rotten
Unforgettable, unforgotten
River-smell, and hear the breeze
Sobbing in the little trees.
Say, do the elm-clumps greatly stand
Still guardians of that holy land?
The chestnuts shade, in reverend dream,
The yet unacademic stream?
Is dawn a secret shy and cold
Anadyomene, silver-gold?
And sunset still a golden sea
From Haslingfield to Madingley?

And after, ere the night is born,
Do hares come out about the corn?

Oh, is the water sweet and cool,
Gentle and brown, above the pool?
And laughs the immortal river still
Under the mill, under the mill?
Say, is there Beauty yet to find?
And Certainty? and Quiet kind?
Deep meadows yet, for to forget
The lies, and truths, and pain? … Oh! yet
Stands the Church clock at ten to three?
And is there honey still for tea?

Leslie Coulson

Killed in action, 1916.

FROM THE SOMME

In other days I sang of simple things,
 Of summer dawn, and summer noon and night,
The dewy grass, the dew-wet fairy rings,
  The lark's long golden flight.

Deep in the forest I made melody
 While squirrels cracked their hazel nuts on high,
Or I would cross the wet sand to the sea
  And sing to sea and sky.

When came the silvered silence of the night
 I stole to casements over scented lawns,
And softly sang of love and love's delight
  To mute white marble fauns.

Oft in the tavern parlour I would sing
  Of morning sun upon the mountain vine,
And, calling for a chorus, sweep the string
    In praise of good red wine.

I played with all the toys the gods provide,
  I sang my songs and made glad holiday.
Now I have cast my broken toys aside
    And flung my lute away.

A singer once, I now am fain to weep.
  Within my soul I feel strange music swell,
Vast chants of tragedy too deep – too deep
    For my poor lips to tell.

Ivor Gurney

THE RETREAT

After three weeks of freezing and thawing over
Against Chaulnes, mud dreadful, with water cover
Of gumboots in the low places, and ice of nights,
They marched us out sore footed to far billets,
Straw and warm tea, more bread; letters more ...
Where for a week we recovered; and now less sore
Our feet were – beer there was, a little bread, wine;
But not the strength they asked of making roads fine
With weak bodies, sore feet, and hungry bellies.
Warmth there was, and sleep – the barn a Palace.
When suddenly the news came, Fritz has retreated ...
What! from Chaulnes wired yard-deep – where a shot
  greeted
Any patrol at midnight moving strict ways,
None else to take? It was a most strict terrible maze.
It was true – we marched three days – to our old place,
Passed through a hedge of No Man's Land and saw far
Other lines, pillboxes, headquarters, and further,
Artillery wired positions, Heads of Divisions.

Passed, came to Omiécourt, found billets; it was but the
  fractions
Of farms – but wood in plenty, and water pure,
Fire Warm, billets warm while the North wind sheer
Tore a space round corners of our one small room.
There was a Mass book, great Plainsong in the gloom
Of the broken church with German Journals and such …
I found a score of postcards in a billet, to catch
All of them, and to be sorry afterwards …
But first finding den and souvenirs as rewards.
After that, onward slowly till roads we had mended;
Weak, hungry, feeling the heart labour bended;
To come to the last rise, see Somme azure of blaze
(Soft March … it was warm of sun), and go onwards, across
The pioneer mending of the arch broken; by planking
Laid across, rattling but standing strain, Transport clanking,
Artillery. We passed Y, and another huge, mined,
  destroyed place,
(Terribly huge) and on till Caulaincourt valley of grace.
Home of the dead men, of Napoleon's men
Lay in the Mausoleum, expecting never invasion,
Nor to see Gloucesters guarding a place that few

Should touch, but of the old rule Rousseau or Le Sage
knew –
But Caulaincourt glad enough boys were there who had stuff
Of such within them communion with the smooth and
rough
Of road and valley gleaming with lit sapling water
Young Artois' sister to become Somme's one daughter
Glimmering beauty before 'Lights Out' stirring heart out
To tears. (I climbed weak-kneed, I saw fallow unploughed
And the darling valley …) German prisoners passed,
defiantly:
One gaily: and we went on to artillery before the town,
Vermand, where (road mending) our Captain rode too far
shown
And got a blast of gun barrage – frightened his horse –
A Company
Took Vermand – two prisoners; and our first trophy
A machine-gun … So further to high banks France had raised
Long ago against the Eastward threat, nobly placed
To be the guard of Vermand, Caulaincourt, Somme's Land;
Free men making, cursing arms-taking to Hell out of hand:

Digging with sulky vigour; or in furious paced
Frenzy: promised dismissal and an early end
(We knew). Fine mounds of Roman sort we saw looming
First through the dim night. Then one miserable week,
Through displeasure of the weather, body-sick, heart-sick,
Saw change from green to white, white to golden,
With sleet and sunshine changing, with storm and sun
  frowning.

First night I lay forward freezing, while others dug pits,
A lump of panged ice. Two hours watching keen for Fritz,
Who saw no more than flurries of snow against the spinnies
Or bare ridge … Next day rested, at night advanced
To the near wood, searched and left; nothing but fancies
Of shadows; nothing but dry leaves rustling fortissimo.
Left again, spent one day of before-Spring sun.
But next to be bombarded by Fritz while guarded
Our own feeble guns with a third of such.
So we dug in, under the trunks and brush.
Stayed – in holes – with a sheet to get warmth and shelter
(On which the winter leaves pattered helter skelter,
And the trees dripped.) I was sentry – with two others;
When suddenly, two hundred off, three great Germans

Appeared … the sentry (duty) ran quietly off
To warn the others. His friend went off in the smothers
Of embarrassment … I alone (good shot) in the foreground?
Now, Ivor Gurney lonely, make no sound, wait.
The others are at the wood-end; now waste no shot.
No noise, no noise … To find (as once: a mine)
My equipment tangled up in my right ear: the bayonet
Hurting my ribs; the fore-sight; O where the fore-sight
Against the woods gunmetal, most lovely, shine?
They touched the wood. I fired straight at the middle one.
No move; now at the right side of the left one.
No move; again between the right one and middle one…
When up there dashed my Platoon, crashing branches down;
And off went Germans as swift as deer, as soon
To turn. Great, well-fed men, to our hungry:
Two Corporals; one over-fed, lusty Lance Corporal
I should guess … How did I miss them! How did I miss?
But I refuse to believe (flatly refuse)
And believe that men may be shot through middle bodies
Before enemies without dropping. I, who had hit posts
As hard as ghosts to hit in Verey lights of Laventie …
Posts and any echoing thing … It was, and yet is
Absurd to me to think the belly may not be wholly
Shot through – by a tiny bullet of our Army

And the man not stand up without sign of folly
Or wound … The nicest men I had seen for six
Weeks; to our poor scarecrows of weak pulses …
Moving by will, – hungry, yet comradely;
While these comfortable Burghers came over like country
   squires
To see the work of the farmhand; happy after white coffee;
And a good gossip before glowing half wood fires …
(O! O! Newspapers Anglais, Français Papers daily,
What have you told us of hungry or cowed Bavaria, Saxony?
What yarns of three-course dinners, when here the sinners
Come overland 8 mile an hour, and do it easily?
And walk off indigestion after meals like millionaires
For size (and accomplishment)? O Wurtemburgherie,
Is this the population you fake your figures on?
Is this the beaten horde of conscripts, beginners?
(Two as nice men as I'd ever meet again …)

So we talked over … they cursed me … the little skirmish:
Cursed also and felt excitement and watched them vanish,
Like record-breakers, over the chalk slope borders.

'Goodbye' – 'You-chaps, I'm sure I hit them in the guts.
Bang through or near … You know I have hit dark
posts,
My equipment round my neck …' To which only jests
Were answer; and 'no excuses for a miss at twelve yards, sir!'
Next night to trench again – and they told us we were going
Over the top to take some unseen damned wiring
Over the crest. They bombarded, and our guns cutting were
trying.
At seven the drizzle began; at 10 we formed in Line …
And (they too fast) went over across country,
I grumbling, and half running; while silence sombrely
Hung over all things, the air misty almost rainy,
I weak as a rabbit 'How much longer, dammit?'
They said 'Shut up'. I said 'I wish this were over!'
They said 'Shut up'. When suddenly up went a cheer.
The men on the left had hit it … I stumbled on and struck it
Blind eyed, upfaced … fearing wire high and to be scratch-
faced.
Hit wire, and lay down … seeing fires, whether of theirs
Or ours, cutting the wires I knew not, only from behind

The impatient second line shot past my helmet,
And the machine-guns blazed away, lower, lower
(O Christ, what pain) and lower, till my body did cower
Stuck to the mire, and no holes at all in the wire.
So much for artillery fire …
The Company jester and my little lieutenant
Crept about: snipping odd wires … ten yards I guessed went
Before us (or over ten foot) and shells came down, and that
damned machine-gun
Sprayed us … O down, further down; Vermand,
You are too chalky a land … We retreated … dug shallow
Pits – the moon above the mist made a mellow
Light, transfused – we could see an old machine-gun post …
And nothing more – we were a little down in the hollow.
Again returning, to catch the same – lighter now, see wires
Thick against dares; and no more forrader; to retreat again;
When suddenly my arm went blazing with bright ardour of
pain;
The end of music … I knelt down and cursed the double
Treachery of Fritz to Europe and to English music:
Cursed Pomerania, Saxony, Wurtemburg, Bavaria,

Prussia, Rheinland, Mecklenburg, Pomerania
Again … (But had forgotten Franconia, Swabia)
Then said 'You chaps, she's beginning to move again;'
(Borrowed a rifle – shot one shot to say 'These things were so.
My arm – she'll stay on yet; I believe it's a Blighty.')
And the stretcher-bearers bound it up carefully, neatly …
In the darkness whitely … And I left them all, vulgar soldiers to brawl;
Passed through reserve in the sunken Road … Oxfords I just could
See, who asked me news: 'O wires, wires, wires, sticks, wood …
Machine-guns, machine-guns, shells … Nothing else. Goodnight!'
And went off through a barrage spraying the hill side
(Machine-guns) risking so much … tired out and careless:
Having a Blighty; hunger; weakness; by disgust fearless;
And saw the downward slope to Blighty and new hope.

NEAR VERMAND

Lying flat on my belly shivering in clutch-frost,
There was time to watch the stars, we had dug in:
Looking eastwards over the low ridge; March scurried its blast
At our senses, no use either dying or struggling.
Low woods to left – (Cotswold her spinnies if ever)
Showed through snow flurries and the clearer star weather,
And nothing but chill and wonder lived in mind; nothing
But loathing and fine beauty, and wet loathed clothing.
Here were thoughts. Cold smothering and fire-desiring,
A day to follow like this or in the digging or wiring.

Worry in snow flurry and lying flat, flesh the earth loathing.
I was the forward sentry and would be relieved
In a quarter or so, but nothing more better than to crouch
Low in the scraped holes and to have frozen and rocky couch –
To be by desperate home thoughts clutched at, and heart-
grieved.
Was I ever there – a lit warm room and Bach, to search out sacred
Meaning; and to find no luck; and to take love as believed?

REQUIEM

Pour out your light, O stars, and do not hold
  Your loveliest shining from earth's outworn shell –
Pure and cold your radiance, pure and cold
  My dead friend's face as well.

PAIN

Pain, pain continual; pain unending;
Hard even to the roughest, but to those
Hungry for beauty … Not the wisest knows,
Nor most pitiful-hearted, what the wending
Of one hour's way meant. Grey monotony lending
Weight to the grey skies, grey mud where goes
An army of grey bedrenched scarecrows in rows
Careless at last of cruellest Fate-sending.
Seeing the pitiful eyes of men foredone,
Or horses shot, too tired merely to stir,
Dying in shell-holes both, slain by the mud.
Men broken, shrieking even to hear a gun.
Till pain grinds down, or lethargy numbs her,
The amazed heart cries angrily out on God.

SERVITUDE

If it were not for England, who would bear
This heavy servitude one moment more?
To keep a brothel, sweep and wash the floor
Of filthiest hovels were noble to compare
With this brass-cleaning life. Now here, now there
Harried in foolishness, scanned curiously o'er
By fools made brazen by conceit, and store
Of antique witticisms thin and bare.
Only the love of comrades sweetens all,
Whose laughing spirit will not be outdone.
As night-watching men wait for the sun
To hearten them, so wait I on such boys
As neither brass nor Hell-fire may appal,
Nor guns, nor sergeant-major's bluster and noise.

TO THE POET BEFORE BATTLE

Now, youth, the hour of thy dread passion comes;
Thy lovely things must all be laid away;
And thou, as others, must face the riven day
Unstirred by rattle of the rolling drums,
Or bugles' strident cry. When mere noise numbs
The sense of being, the fear-sick soul doth sway,
Remember thy great craft's honour, that they may say
Nothing in shame of poets. Then the crumbs
Of praise the little versemen joyed to take
Shall be forgotten; then they must know we are,
For all our skill in words, equal in might
And strong of mettle as those we honoured; make
The name of poet terrible in just war,
And like a crown of honour upon the fight.

W.N. Hodgson

Killed in action, 1916.

ENGLAND TO HER SONS

Sons of mine, I hear you thrilling
To the trumpet call of war;
Gird ye then, I give you freely
As I gave your sires before,
All the noblest of the children I in love and anguish bore.

Free in service, wise in justice,
Fearing but dishonour's breath;
Steeled to suffer uncomplaining
Loss and failure, pain and death;
Strong in faith that sees the issue and in hope that
triumpheth.

Go, and may the God of battles
You in His good guidance keep:
And if He in wisdom giveth
Unto His beloved sleep,
I accept it nothing asking, save a little space to weep.

T.M. Kettle

This was written four days before the poet's death in action, 1916.

TO MY DAUGHTER BETTY

In wiser days, my darling rosebud, blown
To beauty proud as was your Mother's prime,
In that desired, delayed, incredible time,
You'll ask why I abandoned you, my own,
And the dear heart that was your baby throne,
To dice with death. And oh! they'll give you rhyme
And reason: some will call the thing sublime,
And some decry it in a knowing tone.
So here, while the mad guns curse overhead,
And tired men sigh with mud for couch and floor,
Know that we fools, now with the foolish dead,
Died not for flag, nor King, nor Emperor,
But for a dream, born in a herdsman's shed,
And for the secret Scripture of the poor.

Rudyard Kipling
Memories

1930

"The eradication of memories of the Great War." – Socialist Government Organ.

The Socialist Government speaks:

Though all the Dead were all forgot
  And razed were every tomb,
The Worm – the Worm that dieth not
  Compels Us to our doom.
Though all which once was England stands
  Subservient to Our will,
The Dead of whom we washed Our hands,
  They have observance still.

We laid no finger to Their load.
  We multiplied Their woes.
We used Their dearly-opened road
  To traffic with Their foes:

And yet to Them men turn their eyes,
  To Them are vows renewed
Of Faith, Obedience, Sacrifice,
  Honour and Fortitude!

Which things must perish. But Our hour
  Comes not by staves or swords
So much as, subtly, through the power
  Of small corroding words.
No need to make the plot more plain
  By any open thrust;
But – see Their memory is slain
  Long ere Their bones are dust!

Wisely, but yearly, filch some wreath –
  Lay some proud rite aside –
And daily tarnish with Our breath
  The ends for which They died.
Distract, deride, decry, confuse –
  (Or – if it serve Us – pray!)
So presently We break the use
  And meaning of Their day!

Francis Ledwidge

Killed in action, 1917.

SOLILOQUY

When I was young I had a care
Lest I should cheat me of my share
Of that which makes it sweet to strive
For life, and dying still survive,
A name in sunshine written higher
Than lark or poet dare aspire.

But I grew weary doing well,
Besides, 'twas sweeter in that hell,
Down with the loud banditti people
Who robbed the orchards, climbed the steeple
For jackdaws' eggs and made the cock
Crow ere 'twas daylight on the clock.
I was so very bad the neighbours
Spoke of me at their daily labours.

And now I'm drinking wine in France,
The helpless child of circumstance.
Tomorrow will be loud with war,
How will I be accounted for?

It is too late now to retrieve
A fallen dream, too late to grieve
A name unmade, but not too late
To thank the gods for what is great;
A keen-edged sword, a soldier's heart,
Is greater than a poet's art.
And greater than a poet's fame
A little grave that has no name.

John McCrae

Died in base hospital, 1918.

from THE ANXIOUS DEAD

O guns, fall silent till the dead men hear
   Above their heads the legions pressing on:
(These fought their fight in time of bitter fear,
   And died not knowing how the day had gone.)

O flashing muzzles, pause, and let them see
   The coming dawn that streaks the sky afar;
Then let your mighty chorus witness be
   To them, and Caesar, that we still make war.

Tell them, O guns, that we have heard their call,
   That we have sworn and will not turn aside,
That we will onward till we win or fall,
   That we will keep the faith for which they died.

Bid them be patient, and some day, anon,
   They shall feel earth enwrapt in silence deep;
Shall greet, in wonderment, the quiet dawn,
   And in content may turn them to their sleep.

IN FLANDERS FIELDS

In Flanders fields the poppies blow
Between the crosses, row on row
   That mark our place; and in the sky
   The larks, still bravely singing, fly
Scarce heard amid the guns below.

We are the Dead. Short days ago
We lived, felt dawn, saw sunset glow,
   Loved and were loved, and now we lie
      In Flanders fields.

Take up our quarrel with the foe:
To you from failing hands we throw
   The torch; be yours to hold it high.
   If ye break faith with us who die
We shall not sleep, though poppies grow
      In Flanders fields.

E.A. Mackintosh

Killed in action, 1917.

IN MEMORIAM

Private D. Sutherland killed in action in the German trench, May 16th, 1916, and the others who died.

So you were David's father,
And he was your only son,
And the new-cut peats are rotting
And the work is left undone,
Because of an old man weeping,
Just an old man in pain,
For David, his son David,
That will not come again.

Oh, the letters he wrote you,
And I can see them still,
Not a word of the fighting
But just the sheep on the hill

And how you should get the crops in
Ere the year get stonnier,
And the Bosches have got his body,
And I was his officer.

You were only David's father,
But I had fifty sons
When we went up in the evening
Under the arch of the guns,
And we came back at twilight –
O God! I heard them call
To me for help and pity
That could not help at all.

Oh, never will I forget you,
My men that trusted me,
More my sons than your fathers',
For they could only see
The little helpless babies
And the young men in their pride.
They could not see you dying,
And hold you while you died.

Happy and young and gallant,
They saw their first-born go,
But not the strong limbs broken
And the beautiful men brought low,
The piteous writhing bodies,
They screamed 'Don't leave me, sir,'
For they were only your fathers
But I was your officer.

John Gillespie Magee

This poem, written by a nineteen-year-old RCAF pilot, killed in 1941, is considered a classic by airmen.

HIGH FLIGHT

Oh, I have slipped the surly bonds of Earth
And danced the skies on laughter-silvered wings;
Sunward I've climbed and joined the tumbling mirth
Of sun-split clouds – and done a hundred things
You have not dreamed of – wheeled and soared and swung
High in the sunlit silence; hovering there,
I've chased the shouting wind along, and flung
My eager craft through footless halls of air.
Up, up the long, delirious burning blue
I've topped the wind-swept heights with easy grace
Where never lark, or even eagle ever flew –
And, while with silent lifting mind I've trod
The high untrespassed sanctity of space,
Put out my hand and touched the face of God.

R.B. Marriott-Watson

Killed in action, 1918.

KISMET

Opal fires in the Western sky
(For that which is written must ever be),
And a bullet comes droning, whining by,
To the heart of a sentry close to me,

For some go early, and some go late
(A dying scream on the evening air)
And who is there that believes in Fate
As a soul goes out in the sunset flare?

Wilfred Owen

Killed in action, 1918.

TO POESY

A thousand suppliants stand around thy throne,
Stricken with love for thee, O Poesy.
I stand among them, and with them I groan,
And stretch my arms for help. Oh, pity me!
No man (save them thou gav'st the right to ascend
And sit with thee, 'nointing with unction fine,
Calling thyself their servant and their friend)
Has loved thee with a purer love than mine.
For, as thou yieldest thy fair self so free
To Masters not a few, so wayward men
Give half their adoration up to thee,
Beseech another goddess guide their pen,
And with another muse their pleasure take.
Not so with me! I neither cease to love,
Nor am content to love but for the sake
Of passing pleasures caught from thee above.
For some will listen to thy trembling voice
Since in its mournful music warbling low,

They hear beloved tunes of long ago.
And some are but enamoured of thy grace
And find it well to kneel to thee, and pray,
Because there oft-times play upon thy face
Smiles of an earthly maiden far away.

INSPECTION

'You! What d'you mean by this?' I rapped.
'You dare come on parade like this?'
'Please, sir, it's –' ''Old yer mouth,' the sergeant
   snapped.
'I takes 'is name, sir?' – 'Please, and then dismiss.'

Some days 'confined to camp' he got,
For being 'dirty on parade'.
He told me, afterwards, the dammèd spot
Was blood, his own. 'Well blood is dirt,' I said.

'Blood's dirt,' he laughed, looking away,
Far off to where his wound had bled
And almost merged for ever into clay.
'The world is washing out its stains,' he said.
'It doesn't like our cheeks so red:
Young blood's its great objection.
But when we're duly white-washed, being dead,
The race will bear Field Marshal God's inspection.'

WITH AN IDENTITY DISC

If ever I had dreamed of my dead name
High in the heart of London, unsurpassed
By Time for ever, and the Fugitive, Fame,
There taking a long sanctuary at last,

I better that; and recollect with shame
How once I longed to hide it from life's heats
Under those holy cypresses, the same
That keep in shade the quiet place of Keats.

Now, rather, thank I God there is no risk
Of gravers scoring it with florid screed,
But let my death be memoried on this disc.
Wear it, sweet friend. Inscribe no date nor deed.
But let thy heart-beat kiss it night and day,
Until the name grow vague and wear away.

ANTHEM FOR DOOMED YOUTH

What passing-bells for these who die as cattle?
  – Only the monstrous anger of the guns.
  Only the stuttering rifles' rapid rattle
Can patter out their hasty orisons.
No mockeries now for them; no prayers nor bells;
  Nor any voice of mourning save the choirs, –
The shrill, demented choirs of wailing shells;
  And bugles calling for them from sad shires.

What candles may be held to speed them all?
  Not in the hands of boys but in their eyes
Shall shine the holy glimmers of goodbyes.
  The pallor of girls' brows shall be their pall;
Their flowers the tenderness of patient minds,
And each slow dusk a drawing-down of blinds.

1914

War broke: and now the Winter of the world
With perishing great darkness closes in.
The foul tornado, centred at Berlin,
Is over all the width of Europe whirled,
Rending the sails of progress. Rent or furled
Are all Art's ensigns. Verse wails. Now begin
Famines of thought and feeling. Love's wine's thin.
The grain of human Autumn rots, down-hurled.

For after Spring had bloomed in early Greece,
And Summer blazed her glory out with Rome,
An Autumn softly fell, a harvest home,
A slow grand age, and rich with all increase.
But now, for us, wild Winter, and the need
Of sowings for new Spring, and blood for seed.

(I SAW HIS ROUND MOUTH'S CRIMSON)

I saw his round mouth's crimson deepen as it fell,
   Like a sun, in his last deep hour;
Watched the magnificent recession of farewell,
   Clouding, half gleam, half glower,
And a last splendour burn the heavens of his cheek.
   And in his eyes
The cold stars lighting, very old and bleak,
   In different skies.

APOLOGIA PRO POEMATE MEO

I, too, saw God through mud, –
  The mud that cracked on cheeks when wretches smiled.
  War brought more glory to their eyes than blood,
  And gave their laughs more glee than shakes a child.

Merry it was to laugh there –
  Where death becomes absurd and life absurder.
  For power was on us as we slashed bones bare
  Not to feel sickness or remorse of murder.

I, too, have dropped off Fear –
  Behind the barrage, dead as my platoon,
  And sailed my spirit surging light and clear
  Past the entanglement where hopes lay strewn;

And witnessed exultation –
  Faces that used to curse me, scowl for scowl,
  Shine and lift up with passion of oblation,
  Seraphic for an hour; though they were foul.

I have made fellowships –
  Untold of happy lovers in old song.
  For love is not the binding of fair lips
  With the soft silk of eyes that look and long,

By Joy, whose ribbon slips, –
  But wound with war's hard wire whose stakes are strong;
  Bound with the bandage of the arm that drips;
  Knit in the webbing of the rifle-thong.

I have perceived much beauty
  In the hoarse oaths that kept our courage straight;
  Heard music in the silentness of duty;
  Found peace where shell-storms spouted reddest spate.

Nevertheless, except you share
  With them in hell the sorrowful dark of hell,
  Whose world is but the trembling of a flare
  And heaven but as the highway for a shell,

You shall not hear their mirth:
  You shall not come to think them well content
  By any jest of mine. These men are worth
  Your tears. You are not worth their merriment.

MINERS

There was a whispering in my hearth,
  A sigh of the coal,
Grown wistful of a former earth
  It might recall.

I listened for a tale of leaves
  And smothered ferns,
Frond-forests, and the low sly lives
  Before the fauns.

My fire might show steam-phantoms simmer
  From Time's old cauldron,
Before the birds made nests in summer,
  Or men had children.

But coals were murmuring of their mine,
  And moans down there
Of boys that slept wry sleep, and men
  Writhing for air.

And I saw white bones in the cinder-shard,
  Bones without number.
Many the muscled bodies charred,
  And few remember.

I thought of all that worked dark pits
  Of war, and died
Digging the rock where Death reputes
  Peace lies indeed.

Comforted years will sit soft-chaired,
  In rooms of amber;
The years will stretch their hands, well-cheered
  By our life's ember;

The centuries will burn rich loads
  With which we groaned,
Whose warmth shall lull their dreaming lids,
  While songs are crooned;
But they will not dream of us poor lads,
  Left in the ground.

THE LETTER

With B.E.F. June 10. Dear Wife,
(Oh blast this pencil. 'Ere, Bill, lend's a knife.)
I'm in the pink at present, dear.
I think the war will end this year.
We don't see much of them square-'eaded 'Uns.
We're out of harm's way, not bad fed.
I'm longing for a taste of your old buns.
(Say, Jimmie, spare's a bite of bread.)
There don't seem much to say just now.
(Yer What? Then don't yer ruddy cow!
And give us back me cigarette!)
I'll soon be 'ome. You mustn't fret.
My feet's improvin', as I told you of.
We're out in rest now. Never fear.
(VRACH! By crumbs, but that was near.)
Mother might spare you half a sov.
Kiss Nell and Bert. When me and you –
(Eh? What the 'ell! Stand to? Stand to!
Jim, give's a hand with pack on, lad.
Guh! Christ! I'm hit. Take 'old. Aye, Bad.
No, damn your iodine. Jim? 'Ere!
Write my old girl, Jim, there's a dear.)

CONSCIOUS

His fingers wake, and flutter; up the bed.
His eyes come open with a pull of will,
Helped by the yellow mayflowers by his head.
The blind-cord drawls across the window-sill …
What a smooth floor the ward has! What a rug!
Who is that talking somewhere out of sight?
Three flies are creeping round the shiny jug …
'Nurse! Doctor!' – 'Yes, all right, all right.'

But sudden evening blurs and fogs the air.
There seems no time to want a drink of water.
Nurse looks so far away. And here and there
Music and roses burst through crimson slaughter.
He can't remember where he saw blue sky …
The trench is narrower. Cold, he's cold; yet hot –
And there's not light to see the voices by …
There is no time to ask … he knows not what.

DULCE ET DECORUM EST

Bent double, like old beggars under sacks,
Knock-kneed, coughing like hags, we cursed through sludge,
Till on the haunting flares we turned our backs
And towards our distant rest began to trudge.
Men marched asleep. Many had lost their boots
But limped on, blood-shod. All went lame; all blind;
Drunk with fatigue; deaf even to the hoots
Of tired, outstripped Five-Nines that dropped behind.

Gas! GAS! Quick, boys! – An ecstasy of fumbling,
Fitting the clumsy helmets just in time;
But someone still was yelling out and stumbling,
And flound'ring like a man in fire or lime ...
Dim, through the misty panes and thick green light,
As under a green sea, I saw him drowning.

In all my dreams, before my helpless sight,
He plunges at me, guttering, choking, drowning.

If in some smothering dreams you too could pace
Behind the wagon that we flung him in,
And watch the white eyes writhing in his face,
His hanging face, like a devil's sick of sin;
If you could hear, at every jolt, the blood
Come gargling from the froth-corrupted lungs,
Obscene as cancer, bitter as the cud
Of vile, incurable sores on innocent tongues, –
My friend, you would not tell with such high zest
To children ardent for some desperate glory,
The old Lie: Dulce et decorum est
Pro patria mori.

THE DEAD-BEAT

He dropped, – more sullenly than wearily,
Lay stupid like a cod, heavy like meat,
And none of us could kick him to his feet;
– Just blinked at my revolver, blearily;
– Didn't appear to know a war was on,
Or see the blasted trench at which he stared.
'I'll do 'em in,' he whined. 'If this hand's spared,
I'll murder them, I will.'

A low voice said,

'It's Blighty, p'raps, he sees; his pluck's all gone,
Dreaming of all the valiant, that aren't dead:
Bold uncles, smiling ministerially;
Maybe his brave young wife, getting her fun
In some new home, improved materially.
It's not these stiffs have crazed him; nor the Hun.'

We sent him down at last, out of the way.
Unwounded; – stout lad, too, before that strafe.
Malingering? Stretcher-bearers winked, 'Not half!'

Next day I heard the Doc's well-whiskied laugh:
'That scum you sent last night soon died. Hooray!'

INSENSIBILITY

Happy are men who yet before they are killed
Can let their veins run cold.
Whom no compassion fleers
Or makes their feet
Sore on the alleys cobbled with their brothers.
The front line withers.
But they are troops who fade, not flowers,
For poets' tearful fooling:
Men, gaps for filling:
Losses, who might have fought
Longer; but no one bothers.

And some cease feeling
Even themselves or for themselves.
Dullness best solves
The tease and doubt of shelling,
And Chance's strange arithmetic
Comes simpler than the reckoning of their shilling.
They keep no check on armies' decimation.

Happy are these who lose imagination:
They have enough to carry with ammunition.
Their spirit drags no pack.
Their old wounds, save with cold, can not more ache.
Having seen all things red,
Their eyes are rid
Of the hurt of the colour of blood for ever.
And terror's first constriction over,
Their hearts remain small-drawn.
Their senses in some scorching cautery of battle
Now long since ironed,
Can laugh among the dying, unconcerned.

Happy the soldier home, with not a notion
How somewhere, every dawn, some men attack,
And many sighs are drained.
Happy the lad whose mind was never trained:
His days are worth forgetting more than not.
He sings along the march
Which we march taciturn, because of dusk,
The long, forlorn, relentless trend
From larger day to huger night.

We wise, who with a thought besmirch
Blood over all our soul,
How should we see our task
But through his blunt and lashless eyes?
Alive, he is not vital overmuch;
Dying, not mortal overmuch;
Nor sad, nor proud,
Nor curious at all.
He cannot tell
Old Men's placidity from his.

SONNET

On Seeing a Piece of Our Heavy Artillery
Brought into Action.

Be slowly lifted up, thou long black arm,
Great Gun towering towards Heaven, about to curse;
Sway steep against them, and for years rchearse
Huge imprecations like a blasting charm!
Reach at that Arrogance which needs thy harm,
And beat it down before its sins grow worse.
Spend our resentment, cannon, – yea, disburse
Our gold in shapes in flame, our breaths in storm.

Yet, for men's sakes whom thy vast malison
Must wither innocent of enmity,
Be not withdrawn, dark arm, thy spoilure done,
Safe to the bosom of our prosperity.
But when thy spell be cast complete and whole,
May God curse thee, and cut thee from our soul!

ASLEEP

Under his helmet, up against his pack,
After so many days of work and waking,
Sleep took him by the brow and laid him back.

There, in the happy no-time of his sleeping,
Death took him by the heart. There heaved a quaking
Of the aborted life within him leaping,
Then chest and sleepy arms once more fell slack.

And soon the slow, stray blood came creeping
From the intruding lead, like ants on track.
Whether his deeper sleep lie shaded by the shaking
Of great wings, and the thoughts that hung the stars,
High-pillowed on calm pillows of God's making,
Above these clouds, these rains, these sleets of lead,
And these winds' scimitars,
– Or whether yet his thin and sodden head

Confuses more and more with the low mould,
His hair being one with the grey grass
Of finished fields, and wire-scrags rusty-old,
Who knows? Who hopes? Who troubles? Let it pass!
He sleeps. He sleeps less tremulous, less cold,
Than we who wake, and waking say Alas!

FUTILITY

Move him into the sun –
Gently its touch awoke him once,
At home, whispering of fields half-sown.
Always it woke him, even in France,
Until this morning and this snow.
If anything might rouse him now
The kind old sun will know.

Think how it wakes the seeds –
Woke once the clays of a cold star.
Are limbs, so dear achieved, are sides
Full-nerved, still warm, too hard to stir?
Was it for this the clay grew tall?
– O what made fatuous sunbeams toil
To break earth's sleep at all?

THE END

After the blast of lightning from the east,
  The flourish of loud clouds, the Chariot Throne;
After the drums of time have rolled and ceased,
  And by the bronze west long retreat is blown,
Shall Life renew these bodies? Of a truth,
  All death will he annul, all tears assuage?
Or fill these void veins full again with youth,
  And wash, with an immortal water, age?

When I do ask white Age, he saith not so:
  'My head hangs weighed with snow.'
And when I hearken to the Earth, she saith:
  'My fiery heart shrinks, aching. It is death.
Mine ancient scars shall not be glorified,
  Nor my titanic tears, the seas, be dried.'

S.I.W.

S.I.W. was shorthand for self-inflicted wound – usually a bullet or bayonet in the foot, taken as a last desperate measure to escape the front line.

I The Prologue

Patting goodbye, doubtless they told the lad
He'd always show the Hun a brave man's face;
Father would sooner him dead than in disgrace, –
Was proud to see him going, aye, and glad.
Perhaps his mother whimpered how she'd fret
Until he got a nice safe wound to nurse.
Sisters would wish girls too could shoot, charge, curse …
Brothers – would send his favourite cigarette.
Each week, month after month, they wrote the same,
Thinking him sheltered in some Y. M. Hut,
Because he said so, writing on his butt
Where once an hour a bullet missed its aim.
And misses teased the hunger of his brain.
His eyes grew old with wincing, and his hand
Reckless with ague. Courage leaked, as sand
From the best sandbags after years of rain.
But never leave, wound, fever, trench-foot, shock,
Untrapped the wretch. And death seemed still withheld
For torture of lying machinally shelled,

At the pleasure of this world's Powers who'd run amok.
He'd seen men shoot their hands, on night patrol.
Their people never knew. Yet they were vile.
'Death sooner than dishonour, that's the style!'
So Father said.

II The Action

One dawn, our wire patrol
Carried him. This time, Death had not missed.
We could do nothing but wipe his bleeding cough.
Could it be accident – Rifles go off ...
Not sniped? No. (Later they found the English ball.)

III The Poem

It was the reasoned crisis of his soul
Against more days of inescapable thrall,
Against infrangibly wired and blind trench wall
Curtained with fire, roofed in with creeping fire,
Slow grazing fire, that would not burn him whole
But kept him for death's promises and scoff,
And life's half-promising, and both their riling.

IV The Epilogue

With him they buried the muzzle his teeth had kissed,
And truthfully wrote the mother, 'Tim died smiling.'

THE SENTRY

We'd found an old Boche dug-out, and he knew,
And gave us hell, for shell on frantic shell
Hammered on top, but never quite burst through.
Rain, guttering down in waterfalls of slime,
Kept slush waist high that, rising hour by hour,
Choked up the steps too thick with clay to climb.
What murk of air remained stank old, and sour
With fumes of whizz-bangs, and the smell of men
Who'd lived there years, and left their curse in the den,
If not their corpses ...
                                        There we herded from the blast
Of whizz-bangs, but one found our door at last.
Buffeting eyes and breath, snuffing the candles,
And thud! flump! thud! down the steep steps came thumping
And sploshing in the flood, deluging muck –
The sentry's body; then his rifle, handles
Of old Boche bombs, and mud in ruck on ruck.
We dredged him up, for killed, until he whined
'O sir, my eyes – I'm blind – I'm blind, I'm blind!'
Coaxing, I held a flame against his lids
And said if he could see the least blurred light

He was not blind; in time he'd get all right.
'I can't,' he sobbed. Eyeballs, huge-bulged like squids',
Watch my dreams still; but I forgot him there
In posting next for duty, and sending a scout
To beg a stretcher somewhere, and floundering about
To other posts under the shrieking air.

Those other wretches, how they bled and spewed,
And one who would have drowned himself for good, –
I try not to remember these things now:
Let dread hark back for one word only: how
Half-listening to that sentry's moans and jumps,
And the wild chattering of his broken teeth,
Renewed most horribly whenever crumps
Pummelled the roof and slogged the air beneath –
Through the dense din, I say, we heard him shout
'I see your lights!' But ours had long died out.

STRANGE MEETING

It seemed that out of battle I escaped
Down some profound dull tunnel, long since scooped
Through granites which titanic wars had groined.
Yet also there encumbered sleepers groaned,
Too fast in thought or death to be bestirred.
Then, as I probed them, one sprang up, and stared
With piteous recognition in fixed eyes,
Lifting distressful hands as if to bless.
And by his smile, I knew that sullen hall,
By his dead smile I knew we stood in Hell.
With a thousand pains that vision's face was grained;
Yet no blood reached there from the upper ground,
And no guns thumped, or down the flues made moan.'
'Strange friend,' I said, 'here is no cause to mourn.'
'None,' said the other, 'save the undone years,
The hopelessness. Whatever hope is yours,
Was my life also; I went hunting wild
After the wildest beauty in the world,
Which lies not calm in eyes, or braided hair,
But mocks the steady running of the hour,
And if it grieves, grieves richlier than here.
For by my glee might many men have laughed,

And of my weeping something had been left,
Which must die now. I mean the truth untold,
The pity of war, the pity war distilled.
Now men will go content with what we spoiled.
Or, discontent, boil bloody, and be spilled.
They will be swift with swiftness of the tigress,
None will break ranks, though nations trek from progress.
Courage was mine, and I had mystery;
Wisdom was mine, and I had mastery;
To miss the march of this retreating world
Into vain citadels that are not walled.
Then, when much blood had clogged their chariot-wheels
I would go up and wash them from sweet wells,
Even with truths that lie too deep for taint.
I would have poured my spirit without stint
But not through wounds; not on the cess of war.
Foreheads of men have bled where no wounds were.
I am the enemy you killed, my friend.
I knew you in this dark; for so you frowned
Yesterday through me as you jabbed and killed.
I parried; but my hands were loath and cold.
Let us sleep now ...'

Nowell Oxland

Killed in action, Gallipoli, 1915.

OUTWARD BOUND

There's a waterfall I'm leaving
Running down the rocks in foam,
There's a pool for which I'm grieving
Near the water-ouzel's home,
And it's there that I'd be lying
With the heather close at hand,
And the curlews faintly crying
Mid the wastes of Cumberland.

While the midnight watch is winging
Thoughts of other days arise,
I can hear the river singing
Like the Saints in Paradise;
I can see the water winking
Like the merry eyes of Pan,
And the slow half-pounder sinking
By the bridge's granite span.

Ah! to win them back and clamber
Braced anew with winds I love,
From the river's stainless amber
To the morning mist above,
See through cloud-rifts rent asunder
Like a painted scroll unfurled,
Ridge and hollow rolling under
To the fringes of the world.

Now the weary guard are sleeping,
Now the great propellers churn,
Now the harbour lights are creeping
Into emptiness astern,
While the sentry wakes and watches
Plunging triangles of light
Where the water leaps and catches
At our escort in the night.

Great their happiness who seeing
Still with unbenighted eyes
Kin of theirs who gave them being,
Sun and earth that made them wise,
Die and feel their embers quicken
Year by year in summer time,
When the cotton grasses thicken
On the hills they used to climb.

Shall we also be as they be,
Mingled with our mother clay,
Or return no more it may be?
Who has knowledge, who shall say?
Yet we hope that from the bosom
Of our shaggy father Pan,
When the earth breaks into blossom
Richer from the dust of man,

Though the high Gods smite and slay us,
Though we come not whence we go,
As the host of Menelaus
Came there many years ago;
Yet the self-same wind shall bear us
From the same departing place
Out across the Gulf of Saros
And the peaks of Samothrace;

We shall pass in summer weather,
We shall come at eventide,
When the fells stand up together
And all quiet things abide;

Mixed with cloud and wind and river,
Sun-distilled in dew and rain,
One with Cumberland for ever
We shall go not forth again.

Robert Palmer

Killed in action, 1916.

HOW LONG, O LORD?

How long, O Lord, how long, before the flood
Of crimson-welling carnage shall abate?
From sodden plains in West and East the blood
Of kindly men streams up in mists of hate,
Polluting Thy clean air: and nations great
In reputation of the arts that bind
The world with hopes of Heaven, sink to the state
Of brute barbarians, whose ferocious mind
Gloats o'er the bloody havoc of their kind,
Not knowing love or mercy. Lord, how long
Shall Satan in high places lead the blind
To battle for the passions of the strong?
Oh, touch Thy children's hearts, that they may know
Hate their most hateful, pride their deadliest foe.

Isaac Rosenberg

Killed in action, 1918.

THE DYING SOLDIER

'Here are houses,' he moaned,
'I could reach, but my brain swims.'
Then they thundered and flashed,
And shook the earth to its rims.

'They are gunpits,' he gasped,
'Our men are at the guns.
Water! ... Water! ... Oh, water!
For one of England's dying sons.'

'We cannot give you water,
Were all England in your breath.'
'Water! ... Water! ... Oh, water!'
He moaned and swooned to death.

Louse Hunting

Lice were a fact of life in the trenches, where even basic cleanliness was impossible to manage.

NUDES – stark and glistening,
Yelling in lurid glee. Grinning faces
And raging limbs
Whirl over the floor one fire.
For a shirt verminously busy
Yon soldier tore from his throat, with oaths
Godhead might shrink at, but not the lice.
And soon the shirt was aflare
Over the candle he'd lit while we lay.

Then we all sprang up and stript
To hunt the verminous brood.
Soon like a demons' pantomime
The place was raging.
See the silhouettes agape,
See the gibbering shadows
Mixed with the battled arms on the wall.
See gargantuan hooked fingers

Pluck in supreme flesh
To smutch supreme littleness.
See the merry limbs in hot Highland fling
Because some wizard vermin
Charmed from the quiet this revel
When our ears were half lulled
By the dark music
Blown from Sleep's trumpet.

Break of Day in the Trenches

Soldiers shared a love/hate relationship with the hordes of rats that infested the vast network of trenches and travelled freely across No Man's Land.

The darkness crumbles away –
It is the same old druid Time as ever.
Only a live thing leaps my hand –
A queer sardonic rat –
As I pull the parapet's poppy
To stick behind my ear.
Droll rat, they would shoot you if they knew
Your cosmopolitan sympathies.
Now you have touched this English hand
You will do the same to a German –
Soon, no doubt, if it be your pleasure
To cross the sleeping green between.
It seems you inwardly grin as you pass
Strong eyes, fine limbs, haughty athletes
Less chanced than you for life,
Bonds to the whims of murder,
Sprawled in the bowels of the earth,
The torn fields of France.

What do you see in our eyes
At the shrieking iron and flame
Hurled through still heavens?
What quaver – what heart aghast?
Poppies whose roots are in man's veins
Drop, and are ever dropping;
But mine in my ear is safe,
Just a little white with the dust.

ON RECEIVING NEWS OF THE WAR

Snow is a strange white word.
No ice or frost
Has asked of bud or bird
For Winter's cost.

Yet ice and frost and snow
From earth to sky
This Summer land doth know.
No man knows why.

In all men's hearts it is.
Some spirit old
Hath turned with malign kiss
Our lives to mould.

Red fangs have torn His face.
God's blood is shed.
He mourns from His lone place
His children dead.

O! ancient crimson curse!
Corrode, consume.
Give back this universe
Its pristine bloom.

Siegfried Sassoon

Sassoon survived the war. It gave him a fierce hatred of the military. He edited Wilfred Owen's work after the war.

DIED OF WOUNDS

His wet white face and miserable eyes
Brought nurses to him more than groans and sighs:
But hoarse and low and rapid rose and fell
His troubled voice: he did the business well.

The ward grew dark; but he was still complaining
And calling out for 'Dickie'. 'Curse the Wood!
It's time to go. O Christ, and what's the good?
We'll never take it, and it's always raining.'

I wondered where he'd been; then heard him shout,
'They snipe like hell! O Dickie, don't go out' …
I fell asleep … Next morning he was dead;
And some Slight Wound lay smiling on the bed.

TRENCH DUTY

Shaken from sleep, and numbed and scarce awake,
Out in the trench with three hours' watch to take,
I blunder through the splashing mirk; and then
Hear the gruff muttering voices of the men
Crouching in cabins candle-chinked with light.

Hark! There's the big bombardment on our right
Rumbling and bumping; and the dark's a glare
Of flickering horror in the sectors where
We raid the Boche; men waiting, stiff and chilled,
Or crawling on their bellies through the wire.
'What? Stretcher-bearers wanted? Someone killed?'
Five minutes ago I heard a sniper fire:
Why did he do it? ... Starlight overhead –
Blank stars. I'm wide-awake; and some chap's dead.

THE GENERAL

'Good-morning; good-morning!' the General said
When we met him last week on our way to the line.
Now the soldiers he smiled at are most of 'em dead,
And we're cursing his staff for incompetent swine.
'He's a cheery old card,' grunted Harry to Jack
As they slogged up to Arras with rifle and pack.

But he did for them both by his plan of attack.

THE DUG-OUT

Why do you lie with your legs ungainly huddled,
And one arm bent across your sullen, cold,
Exhausted face? It hurts my heart to watch you,
Deep-shadow'd from the candle's guttering gold;
And you wonder why I shake you by the shoulder;
Drowsy, you mumble and sigh and turn your head ...
You are too young to fall asleep for ever;
And when you sleep you remind me of the dead.

TO ANY DEAD OFFICER

Well, how are things in Heaven? I wish you'd say,
  Because I'd like to know that you're all right.
Tell me, have you found everlasting day,
  Or been sucked in by everlasting night?
For when I shut my eyes your face shows plain;
  I hear you make some cheery old remark –
I can rebuild you in my brain,
  Though you've gone out patrolling in the dark.

You hated tours of trenches; you were proud
  Of nothing more than having good years to spend;
Longed to get home and join the careless crowd
  Of chaps who work in peace with Time for friend.
That's all washed out now. You're beyond the wire:
  No earthly chance can send you crawling back;
You've finished with machine-gun fire –
  Knocked over in a hopeless dud-attack.

Somehow I always thought you'd get done in,
  Because you were so desperate keen to live:
You were all out to try and save your skin,
  Well knowing how much the world had got to give.
You joked at shells and talked the usual 'shop',
  Stuck to your dirty job and did it fine:
With 'Jesus Christ! when *will* it stop?
  Three years ... It's hell unless we break their line.'

So when they told me you'd been left for dead
  I wouldn't believe them, feeling it must be true.
Next week the bloody Roll of Honour said
  'Wounded and missing' – (That's the thing to do
When lads are left in shell-holes dying slow,
  With nothing but blank sky and wounds that ache,
Moaning for water till they know
  It's night, and then it's not worth while to wake!)

Good-bye, old lad! Remember me to God,
  And tell Him that our politicians swear
They won't give in till Prussian Rule's been trod
  Under the Heel of England … Are you there? …
Yes … and the War won't end for at least two years;
  But we've got stacks of men … I'm blind with tears,
Staring into the dark. Cheerio!
  I wish they'd killed you in a decent show.

PRELUDE: THE TROOPS

Dim, gradual thinning of the shapeless gloom
Shudders to drizzling daybreak that reveals
Disconsolate men who stamp their sodden boots
And turn dulled, sunken faces to the sky
Haggard and hopeless. They, who have beaten down
The stale despair of night, must now renew
Their desolation in the truce of dawn,
Murdering the livid hours that grope for peace.

Yet these, who cling to life with stubborn hands,
Can grin through storms of death and find a gap
In the clawed, cruel tangles of his defence.
They march from safety, and the bird-sung joy
Of grass-green thickets, to the land where all
Is ruin, and nothing blossoms but the sky
That hastens over them where they endure
Sad, smoking, flat horizons, reeking woods,
And foundered trench-lines volleying doom for doom.

O my brave brown companions, when your souls
Flock silently away, and the eyeless dead
Shame the wild beast of battle on the ridge,
Death will stand grieving in that field of war
Since your unvanquished hardihood is spent.
And through some mooned Valhalla there will pass
Battalions and battalions, scarred from hell;
The unreturning army that was youth;
The legions who have suffered and are dust.

EVERYONE SANG

Everyone suddenly burst out singing;
And I was filled with such delight
As prisoned birds must find in freedom
Wingіng wildly across the white
Orchards and dark-green fields; on; on; and out
of sight.

Everyone's voice was suddenly lifted,
And beauty came like the setting sun.
My heart was shaken with tears; and horror
Drifted away ... O but every one
Was a bird; and the song was wordless; the
singing will never be done.

TWELVE MONTHS AFTER

Hullo! here's my platoon, the lot I had last year.
'The war'll be over soon.'
  'What 'opes?'
    'No bloody fear!'
Then, 'Number Seven, 'shun! All present and correct.'
They're standing in the sun, impassive and erect.
Young Gibson with his grin; and Morgan, tired and white;
Jordan, who's out to win a D.C.M. some night;
And Hughes that's keen on wiring; and Davies ('79),
Who always must be firing at the Boche front line.

*

'Old soldiers never die; they simply fide a-why!'
That's what they used to sing along the roads last spring;
That's what they used to say before the push began;
That's where they are today, knocked over to a man.

BASE DETAILS

If I were fierce, and bald, and short of breath,
  I'd live with scarlet Majors at the Base,
And speed glum heroes up the line to death.
  You'd see me with my puffy petulant face,
Guzzling and gulping in the best hotel,
  Reading the Roll of Honour. 'Poor young chap,'

I'd say – 'I used to know his father well;
  Yes, we've lost heavily in this last scrap.'
And when the war is done and youth stone dead,
  I'd toddle safely home and die – in bed.

Alan Seeger

Killed in action, 1916.

RENDEZVOUS

I have a rendezvous with Death
At some disputed barricade,
When Spring comes back with rustling shade
And apple-blossoms fill the air –
I have a rendezvous with Death
When Spring brings back blue days and fair.

It may be he shall take my hand
And lead me into his dark land
And close my eyes and quench my breath –
It may be I shall pass him still.
I have a rendezvous with Death
On some scarred slope of battered hill,
When Spring comes round again this year
And the first meadow-flowers appear.

God knows 'twere better to be deep
Pillowed in silk and scented down,
Where love throbs out in blissful sleep,
Pulse nigh to pulse, and breath to breath,
Where hushed awakenings are dear …
But I've a rendezvous with Death
At midnight in some flaming town,
When Spring trips north again this year,
And I to my pledged word am true,
I shall not fail that rendezvous.

Patrick Shaw–Stewart

Killed in action, Pas-de-Calais, 1917.

UNTITLED

I saw a man this morning
  Who did not wish to die:
I ask, and cannot answer,
  If otherwise wish I.

Fair broke the day this morning
  Against the Dardanelles;
The breeze blew soft, the morn's cheeks
  Were cold as cold sea-shells.

But other shells are waiting
  Across the Aegean Sea,
Shrapnel and high explosive,
  Shells and hells for me.

O hell of ships and cities,
   Hell of men like me,
Fatal second Helen,
   Why must I follow thee?

Achilles came to Troyland
   And I to Chersonese:
He turned from wrath to battle,
   And I from three days' peace.

Was it so hard, Achilles,
   So very hard to die?
Thou knowest and I know not –
   So much the happier am I.

I will go back this morning
   From Imbros over the sea;
Stand in the trench, Achilles,
   Flame-capped, and shout for me.

Charles Sorley

Killed in action, 1915.

ALL THE HILLS AND VALES ALONG

All the hills and vales along,
Earth is bursting into song,
And the singers are the chaps
Who are going to die perhaps.
  O sing, marching men,
  Till the valleys ring again.
  Give your gladness to earth's keeping,
  So be glad, when you are sleeping.

Cast away regret and rue,
Think what you are marching to.
Little live, great pass.
Jesus Christ and Barabbas
Were found the same day.
This died, that went his way
  So sing with joyful breath,
  For why, you are going to death.
  Teeming earth will surely store
  All the gladness that you pour.

Earth that never doubts nor fears,
Earth that knows of death, not tears,
Earth that bore with joyful ease
Hemlock for Socrates,
Earth that blossomed and was glad
'Neath the cross that Christ had,
Shall rejoice and blossom too
When the bullet reaches you.
  Wherefore, men marching
  On the road to death, sing!
  Pour your gladness on earth's head,
  So be merry, so be dead.

From the hills and valleys earth
Shouts back the sound of mirth,
Tramp of feet and lilt of song
Ringing all the road along.
All the music of their going,
Ringing swinging glad song-throwing,
Earth will echo still, when foot
Lies numb and voice mute.

On, marching men, on
To the gates of death with song.
Sow your gladness for earth's reaping,
So you may be glad, though sleeping.
Strew your gladness on earth's bed,
So be merry, so be dead.

Edward Thomas

Killed at Arras, 1917.

TEARS

It seems I have no tears left. They should have fallen –
Their ghosts, if tears have ghosts, did fall – that day
When twenty hounds streamed by me, not yet combed out
But still all equals in their rage of gladness
Upon the scent, made one, like a great dragon
In Blooming Meadow that bends towards the sun
And once bore hops: and on that other day
When I stepped out from the double-shadowed Tower
Into an April morning, stirring and sweet
And warm. Strange solitude was there and silence.
A mightier charm than any in the Tower
Possessed the courtyard. They were changing guard,
Soldiers in line, young English countrymen,
Fair-haired and ruddy, in white tunics. Drums
And fifes were playing 'The British Grenadiers'.
The men, the music piercing that solitude
And silence, told me truths I had not dreamed,
And have forgotten since their beauty passed.

A PRIVATE

This ploughman dead in battle slept out of doors
Many a frosty night, and merrily
Answered staid drinkers, good bedmen, and all bores:
'At Mrs Greenland's Hawthorn Bush,' said he,
'I slept.' None knew which bush. Above the town,
Beyond 'The Drover', a hundred spot the down
In Wiltshire. And where now at last he sleeps
More sound in France – that, too, he secret keeps.

SNOW

In the gloom of whiteness,
In the great silence of snow,
A child was sighing
And bitterly saying: 'Oh,
They have killed a white bird up there on her nest,
The down is fluttering from her breast.'
And still it fell through that dusky brightness
On the child crying for the bird of the snow.

NO ONE CARES LESS THAN I

'No one cares less than I,
Nobody knows but God,
Whether I am destined to lie
Under a foreign clod,'
Were the words I made to the bugle call in the morning.

But laughing, storming, scorning,
Only the bugles know
What the bugles say in the morning,
And they do not care, when they blow
The call that I heard and made words to early this morning.

LIGHTS OUT

I have come to the borders of sleep,
The unfathomable deep
Forest where all must lose
Their way, however straight,
Or winding, soon or late;
They cannot choose.

Many a road and track
That, since the dawn's first crack,
Up to the forest brink,
Deceived the travellers,
Suddenly now blurs,
And in they sink.

Here love ends,
Despair, ambition ends;
All pleasure and all trouble,
Although most sweet or bitter,
Here ends in sleep that is sweeter
Than tasks most noble.

There is not any book
Or face of dearest look
That I would not turn from now
To go into the unknown
I must enter, and leave, alone,
I know not how.

The tall forest towers;
Its cloudy foliage lowers
Ahead, shelf above shelf;
Its silence I hear and obey
That I may lose my way
And myself.

AS THE TEAM'S HEAD-BRASS

As the team's head-brass flashed out on the turn
The lovers disappeared into the wood.
I sat among the boughs of the fallen elm
That strewed the angle of the fallow, and
Watched the plough narrowing a yellow square
Of charlock. Every time the horses turned
Instead of treading me down, the ploughman leaned
Upon the handles to say or ask a word,
About the weather, next about the war.
Scraping the share he faced towards the wood,
And screwed along the furrow till the brass flashed
Once more.
                    The blizzard felled the elm whose crest
I sat in, by a woodpecker's round hole,
The ploughman said. 'When will they take it away?'
'When the war's over.' So the talk began –
One minute and an interval of ten,
A minute more and the same interval.
'Have you been out?' 'No.' 'And don't want to,
   perhaps?'
'If I could only come back again, I should.
I could spare an arm. I shouldn't want to lose

A leg. If I should lose my head, why, so,
I should want nothing more … Have many gone
From here?' 'Yes.' 'Many lost?' 'Yes, a good few.
Only two teams work on the farm this year.
One of my mates is dead. The second day
In France they killed him. It was back in March,
The very night of the blizzard, too. Now if
He had stayed here we should have moved the tree.'
'And I should not have sat here. Everything
Would have been different. For it would have been
Another world.' 'Ay, and a better, though
If we could see all all might seem good.' Then
The lovers came out of the wood again:
The horses started and for the last time
I watched the clods crumble and topple over
After the ploughshare and the stumbling team.

THAW

Over the land freckled with snow half-thawed
The speculating rooks at their nests cawed
And saw from elm-tops, delicate as flower of grass,
What we below could not see, Winter pass.

GONE, GONE AGAIN

Gone, gone again,
May, June, July,
And August gone,
Again gone by,

Not memorable
Save that I saw them go,
As past the empty quays
The rivers flow.

And now again,
In the harvest rain,
The Blenheim oranges
Fall grubby from the trees

As when I was young –
And when the lost one was here –
And when the war began
To turn the young men to dung.

Look at the old house,
Outmoded, dignified,
Dark and untenanted,
With grass growing instead

Of the footsteps of life,
The friendliness, the strife;
In its beds have lain
Youth, love, age, and pain:

I am something like that;
Only I am not dead,
Still breathing and interested
In the house that is not dark: –

I am something like that:
Not one pane to reflect the sun,
For the school boys to throw at –
They have broken every one.

R.E. Vernede

Killed in action, 1917.

A LISTENING POST

The sun's a red ball in the oak
  And all the grass is grey with dew,
Awhile ago a blackbird spoke –
  He didn't know the world's askew.

And yonder rifleman and I
  Wait here behind the misty trees
To shoot the first man that goes by,
  Our rifles ready on our knees.

How could he know that if we fail
  The world may lie in chains for years
And England be a bygone tale
  And right be wrong, and laughter tears?

Strange that this bird sits there and sings
   While we must only sit and plan –
Who are so much the higher things –
   The murder of our fellow man …

But maybe God will cause to be –
   Who brought forth sweetness from the strong –
Out of our discords harmony
   Sweeter than that bird's song.

W.B. Yeats

W.B. Yeats wrote this poem in memory of his close friend, Major Robert Gregory, RFC.

AN IRISH AIRMAN FORESEES HIS DEATH

I know that I shall meet my fate
Somewhere among the clouds above;
Those that I fight I do not hate,
Those that I guard I do not love;
My country is Kiltartan Cross,
My countrymen Kiltartan's poor;
No likely end could bring them loss
Or leave them happier than before.
Nor law, nor duty bade me fight,
Nor public men, nor cheering crowds,
A lonely impulse of delight
Drove to this tumult in the clouds;
I balanced all, brought all to mind,
The years to come seemed waste of breath,
A waste of breath the years behind,
In balance with this life, this death.

ON BEING ASKED FOR A WAR POEM

I think it better that in times like these
A poet's mouth be silent, for in truth
We have no gift to set a statesman right;
He has had enough of meddling who can please
A young girl in the indolence of her youth,
Or an old man upon a winter's night.